Harm, Healing, and Human Dignity

A Catholic Encounter with Restorative Justice

Adapted by

Caitlin Morneau

LITURGICAL PRESS

Collegeville, Minnesota

www.litpress.org

1   2   3   4   5   6   7   8   9

Library of Congress Cataloging-in-Publication Data

Names: Morneau, Caitlin, adapter.
Title: Harm, healing, and human dignity : a Catholic encounter with restorative justice / adapted by Caitlin Morneau.
Description: Collegeville : Liturgical Press, 2019.
Identifiers: LCCN 2018052623 (print) | LCCN 2019011425 (ebook) | ISBN 9780814664414 (eBook) | ISBN 9780814664162 (pbk.)
Subjects: LCSH: Restorative justice—Religious aspects—Christianity. | Catholic Church—Doctrines.
Classification: LCC BX1795.J87 (ebook) | LCC BX1795.J87 H37 2019 (print) | DDC 261.8—dc23
LC record available at https://lccn.loc.gov_2018052623

"*Harm, Healing, and Human Dignity* allows the reader to come to a fuller understanding of how restorative justice and Catholic social teaching embrace one another in a way that leads to the creation of communities of hope. It helps us to see beyond the pain and trauma to the possibilities of a life that has meaning and purpose."

—Fr. David Kelly, CPPS
Precious Blood Ministry of Reconciliation

This book was made possible with support from:

The ACTA Foundation
Mundelein, IL

and

Catholic Mobilizing Network,
the national Catholic organization that seeks to end
the death penalty
and promote restorative justice.
Washington, DC

Contents

Preface

Why This Book?

The journey toward restorative justice is one of both heart and mind. Over and over, it asks us to choose healing over vengeance, regardless of the setting. Restorative justice and its practices are far from a simple theory or approach. It is not "soft on crime" or an "easy way out" when addressing harm and violence. We succeed at restorative justice when we learn to foster healing, transform relationships, and build a culture of life. As Scripture tells us, this is a central tenet of our faith: living in right relationship by "lov[ing] your neighbor as yourself" (Mt 22:36-40).

In 2017, Catholic Mobilizing Network and Mount St. Mary's University worked in collaboration with Liturgical Press to publish *Redemption and Restoration: A Catholic Perspective on Restorative Justice*. Its call for Catholics to adopt restorative practices was well received. The book you hold in your hands was adapted from this original text, intending to provide a more user-friendly guide for a wider audience and to serve as a faith formation resource for groups and individuals as they explore the richness of restorative justice. For greater depth *Redemption and Restoration* remains a key resource. This book, *Harm, Healing, and Human Dignity*, illuminates the value of restorative practices for all of us.

Why Now?

Everyone reading this book is directly and indirectly impacted by harm and brokenness through our relationships, ministry, work, and loss. Each one of us has brokenness. We live in a world of division, at a time when the topics of mass incarceration, racial tensions, the #MeToo movement, and the horrors of the sexual abuse crisis in the church are at a boiling point. Political discourse in the public square is nothing if not tense, as evidenced by seemingly endless power-seeking, demonizing, and retribution. One need not look very far to find sin and brokenness around us. Restorative practices can be a path toward healing and modeling Jesus' reconciling way with our lives. Creating communities of inclusion, equity, and civility—which seek to live in right relationships and adhere to the biblical command to love your neighbor—requires all of us.

Catholic Mobilizing Network (CMN) hopes to educate Catholic communities about restorative justice, and provide a leaven for restorative solutions, particularly in the criminal justice system. CMN is a national organization that mobilizes Catholics and all people of goodwill to value life over death, to end the use of the death penalty, to transform the US criminal justice system from punitive to restorative, and to build capacity in US society to engage in restorative practices. From CMN's inception, restorative justice has been key to the identity of the organization—not a secondary endeavor, but rather a fully integrated, core component of CMN's mission.

Faithfully Moving Forward

The dignity of every human person is central to Catholic Church doctrine. Each person is created in the image and likeness of God; all human life is sacred. Pope Francis has made abundantly clear during his pontificate that the treatment of those in prison—especially those on death row—holds a special significance. He has advocated repeatedly for the end of the death penalty, most famously declaring the need to protect life at all stages in front of the United States Congress in September 2015. More recently, in August of 2018, through the Congregation for the Doctrine of the Faith, Pope Francis revised the Catechism to say that use of the death penalty is "inadmissible" in all cases, reaffirming our faith in the power of hope over death. Ultimately, restorative justice seeks to rebuild and restore damaged relationships and is deeply in line with Catholic values and tradition.

Responding to Pope Francis's call to mercy and encounter, this book is an invitation to consider our individual and communal responses to harm and crime, and to reflect on how our criminal justice system falls short of promoting truth, healing, and reconciliation. Through Scripture, personal stories, and eye-opening statistics, each chapter encourages prayerful contemplation about ways to elevate human dignity and principles of Catholic social teaching when responding to crime, incarceration, and the use of the death penalty in the United States.

Restorative justice tradition is rich, and its origins are found in the traditions of our indigenous brothers and sisters whose communities embody its practices to live in right and harmonious relationship with one another. Today, some of the most compelling witnesses to the power of restorative justice include courageous murder victim family members who have suffered grave loss and decided to stand for the dignity of all life and on the side of hope.

Catholic Mobilizing Network envisioned this book to aid in the formation of missionary disciples who incorporate restorative justice principles and practices into their personal,

parish, and community lives, and advocate to transform the
criminal justice system into one that heals and restores. The
online reader guide companion to this book invites you to
learn and listen to restorative justice practitioners and participants (www.catholicsmobilizing.org/rj-reader-guide).

It is often said that hurt people hurt people. But there
is joy in knowing that the converse is equally true: trans-
formed people can and will help transform broken systems
and structures, even one so deeply broken as our current
criminal justice system. This book highlights the importance
of walking with all those impacted by harm and violence.
This is our common journey.

Krisanne Vaillancourt Murphy, Executive Director,
  Catholic Mobilizing Network

Karen Clifton, Founder and Board Member,
  Catholic Mobilizing Network

Chapter 1

When We Think about Justice

> [That God] is there even before the human sinner, waiting and offering him his forgiveness, thus reveals a higher justice which is, at the same time impartial and compassionate, without contradiction in these two aspects. Forgiveness, in fact, neither eliminates nor diminishes the need for correction, precisely that of justice, nor does it overlook the need for personal conversion, instead it goes further, seeking to reestablish relationships and reintegrate people into society.[1]

These are the words of our Holy Father Pope Francis professing the nature of God's justice and mercy. The wisdom he offers is a lot to take in at first glance. It raises a number of questions, too. How can you be impartial and compassionate at the same time? What does it take to reestablish relationships that are broken? What does forgiveness have to do with justice? Come to think of it, what is "justice" anyway? These are questions that have deep meaning in day-to-day life. They also have major consequences for society at large, especially in matters of criminal justice.

In the United States over two million people live behind bars; people who are poor and marginalized are disproportionately represented among individuals who are incarcerated.[2] Families are separated, communities are broken, and countless people are haunted by the memories of violence they experienced. Meanwhile, each year billions of dollars[3] are spent on judicial and correctional systems that, as you will read, often bring further suffering instead of healing and prevention.

For some of us, these national trends are not simple statistics; they are the stories of people we know and love. If we have suffered violence, are currently or formerly incarcerated, or are working in the field of law enforcement or corrections, these are not just facts, but lived experience. We cry with families recovering from a traumatic event or the loss of a loved one. We know the challenges of life inside of prison. We see firsthand when people touched by the criminal justice system are treated as though they are less than human.

For others of us, these numbers and images feel more distant. We read stories in the news or see them depicted in movies. We are troubled by what we see on social media. We feel there must be another way to respond when a law is broken, but it is difficult to imagine what that might look like. After all, the current reality is the only one we've known.

No matter where you fall on this spectrum, you can probably remember a time when you felt wronged by someone in one form or another, big or small, intended or accidental. Since you were drawn to read this book it is likely in those times of trial, pain, or confusion you turned to your faith for comfort, clarity, and a way forward. Know that you are not alone, and you have come to the right place.

Bringing a Catholic Perspective

Scripture makes clear that every human is created in the image and likeness of God. While not unique to the Catholic tradition, this fundamental belief is core to Catholic doctrine and its social teachings. With this orientation Catholic Mobilizing Network (CMN) was formed in 2009. Working in close collaboration with the United States Conference of Catholic Bishops and living the Spirit of Unity of its sponsor—the Congregation of St. Joseph—CMN has sought an end to the use of the death penalty in the United States. CMN is the national organization mobilizing Catholics and people of goodwill to value life over death, to transform the US criminal justice system from punitive to restorative, and to build capacity in US society to engage in restorative practices.

Countless Americans agree that the criminal justice system is broken and that many aspects of it violate human dignity. As people of faith who understand the sacred value of each human life, we know that those who have caused or been impacted by crime should be treated with dignity. But how do we do this in the face of violence?

Catholics were emboldened by the August 2018 revision to the Catechism declaring the death penalty "inadmissible" in all cases. The words and actions of Pope Francis show us a way of responding to harm and wrongdoing as Jesus did, filled with mercy and connection rather than punishment and isolation. CMN has committed to ending a culture of death and darkness found in the practice of the death penalty by instead promoting a culture of life, healing, and hope. **Restorative justice is a way of responding to harm that focuses on repairing relationships and healing all those who are impacted by crime.** Beautifully aligned with

Gospel values, rooted in indigenous traditions, and applicable in many areas of life, restorative justice offers an approach to crime and suffering that honors human dignity and gives way to redemption. Our Catholic faith calls us to understand restorative justice more deeply and find ways to live it in our everyday lives, our communities, and the criminal justice system.

Redemption and Restoration Book
In 2017, Catholic Mobilizing Network, Mount St. Mary's University, and Liturgical Press published *Redemption and Restoration: A Catholic Perspective on Restorative Justice.* The book offers an in-depth examination of our broken criminal justice system, Catholic theology, and applications of restorative justice. This companion book offers a glimpse of what you will find in *Redemption and Restoration.* If you are intrigued by what you read here, order a copy of *Redemption and Restoration* at www.litpress.org.

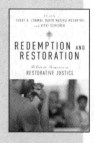

The Challenge of Justice

There are many ways to describe or envision the elusive concept of "justice." Depending on our experiences, we think about it differently. In *Redemption and Restoration,* David Cloutier describes justice as essentially being about what we deserve. One way to think of justice is in terms of "fairness." As children, when we didn't get what we felt we deserved, we cried out "it's not fair!" As adults, we make decisions every day about what we feel someone deserves. A couple of examples include leaving a tip for a server at a restaurant or a teacher grading students' assignments.

In our families, justice becomes more complicated, since there is not a monetary calculation or rubric involved. It is easy to think of fairness as everyone being treated the same, but depending on a child's age, their needs might be different. A teenager will need more to eat than a five-year-old. One child may need a tutor in a particular subject in school, while another might need support socially. So, a spirit of equity considers the particular needs of each person and treats them accordingly.

Human Dignity and God's Vision of Justice

As Catholics, we are compelled by a sense of justice that goes even further than who is "deserving" based on needs. At the end of the day, we believe every person deserves life and love because we have been bestowed God-given dignity. Our Catholic tradition teaches that "human life is sacred because from its beginning it involves the creative action of God and it remains forever in a special relationship with the Creator, who is its sole end."[4] Because of this inherent truth, every person deserves to be treated with dignity, no matter the harm they have suffered or caused. In the 2000 pastoral letter *Responsibility, Rehabilitation, and Restoration: A Catholic Perspective on Crime and Criminal Justice*, the United States Conference of Catholic Bishops said:

> A Catholic approach begins with the recognition that the dignity of the human person applies to both victim and offender. As bishops, we believe that the

current trend of more prisons and more executions, with too little education and drug treatment, does not truly reflect Christian values and will not really leave our communities safer. We are convinced that our tradition and our faith offer better alternatives that can hold offenders accountable *and* challenge them to change their lives; reach out to victims *and* reject vengeance; restore a sense of community *and* resist the violence that has engulfed so much of our culture.[5]

Many Catholics are already taking action to change our nation's criminal justice system and the lives of those who are touched by it. Examples of such ministry and advocacy include spiritual accompaniment to incarcerated individuals, prison reentry and job training programs, mentoring children whose parents are incarcerated, teaching about issues of criminal justice in Catholic schools, and legislative policy reform. Others are concerned about the brokenness they see but do not know where to start. As you will read, restorative practices can strengthen these existing efforts and inspire new ways to live our faith in action. **In addition, restorative justice challenges us to question the assumption that punishment is the only way to achieve justice.**

Restorative Justice and Criminal Justice

This grounding in the sacredness of all life is what makes restorative justice so compatible with our faith tradition. **Restorative justice calls us to see crime, and harm in any form, as a violation of people and relationships rather than as solely a violation of law.** When harm occurs, there are far-reaching consequences: emotional, spiritual, physical, material, and communal. Restorative practices seek to address those consequences through encounter that repairs the harm to the greatest extent possible. Throughout this book you will read about examples of these practices in action, but first, let's think about how this approach differs from our traditional criminal justice system.

If this approach already feels familiar, this is likely because it is consistent with Scripture. As Mary Katherine Birge, SSJ, describes in *Redemption and Restoration*, "Jesus begins from the biblical vision of the kingdom of God, whereas our legal system begins from a stance that immediately seeks out whom to hold guilty for the crime."[6] Here is another way to think about it.

The criminal justice system asks three primary questions:

1. What law was broken?
2. Who is guilty?
3. What should their punishment be?

This focus on punishment is the hallmark of a retributive approach to justice. Just retribution, or giving the punishment that is due to violators of the law, is intended to be a facet of criminal justice. In the United States, however, punishment has become the *only* means of justice.

Alternatively, restorative justice asks a different set of questions as Janine Geske outlines in Redemption and Restoration:

1. Who was harmed by what happened?
2. How can we understand the harm caused by the crime?
3. How do we, as a community, go about repairing the harm caused by this crime?[7]

It is easy to see how orienting our hearts and minds around these questions can lead to a place of greater healing for all involved. But how does such healing occur?

Authentic Encounter and Finding a Better Way

> When we live out a spirituality of drawing nearer
> to others and seeking their welfare, our hearts are
> opened wide to the Lord's greatest and most beauti-
> ful gifts. Whenever we encounter another person in
> love, we learn something new about God. Whenever
> our eyes are opened to acknowledge the other, we
> grow in the light of faith and knowledge of God.
> If we want to advance in the spiritual life, then, we
> must constantly be missionaries.[8]

Pope Francis is calling the church to create a culture of encounter, where we go to the margins of society, share sacred presence, and enter into dialogue with those we meet. Restorative practices offer a structure for such encounters to take place when harm has occurred. There are two foundational restorative practices that will be helpful to know about as you journey through this book.

Circles[9] have been used for generations in indigenous communities to address conflict and live in right relationship with one another. In this process, the individuals sit in a circle and pass a talking piece around to designate the speaker. A circle keeper or facilitator prompts a question or topic to which each person is invited to respond when they receive the talking piece. Simple in its concept, this practice helps to create a safe, invitational space where all voices are heard. Circles can be used following an instance of harm, but also for shared reflection, discernment, and community-building.

Precious Blood Center's Peacemaking Circle
Fr. David Kelly is executive director of Precious Blood
Ministry of Reconciliation (PBMR), a restorative justice
ministry in Chicago's South Side. In this video, he explains more about peacemaking circles and how they
make a difference in the lives of youth that PBMR serves.
To watch the video, visit: www.catholicsmobilizing.org
/rj-reader-guide

Victim-offender dialogue[10] is a facilitated meeting that
brings together person(s) responsible for a harm, person(s)
directly affected, family members, and support people.
Together the group explores the impacts of the incident
and what needs to be done to make things right. There are
various approaches to how these dialogues may be structured, but typically, in order to take place, the person who
committed the harm must first take responsibility for the
offense, all parties participate on a voluntary basis, and each
participant goes through a process of individual preparation
before the group gathers. It should be noted that while a
restorative dialogue that involves all three parties (victim,
offender, and community) can be deeply transformative, it
is not always possible and should not be forced if someone
is not ready or willing to participate. As you will read in
chapter 5, there are variations on these practices that involve
only two of these parties, people involved in similar, but
not the same, crimes, or a different form of communication
such as letter writing.

The stories in this book will highlight the use of circles
and victim-offender dialogue in cases of grave harm and
how they were applied in a criminal justice context. In our
world today, there is so much hurting and brokenness. The

opportunities to use restorative practices are endless. May this book offer inspiration and a place for you to start.

Prayer

Lord, I am weary from the weight of brokenness and division in our world, in the criminal justice system, and in my own life. In you I find hope for redemption and know that you will show me a better way, a more restorative way. Guide my path as I seek to be a messenger of mercy, justice, and human dignity for all people, most especially those impacted by crime and the criminal justice system.

Reflection Questions:

1. Take a look back at the questions that the legal system asks. Can you think of ways in which this retributive approach trickles out to other aspects of life? . . . Schools, workplaces, families, friendships?

2. In cases of grave harm, restorative practices are convened by a trained facilitator and follow a particular structure. In other cases, they are much less formal. Can you think of informal ways to go about answering the "restorative questions"?

3. What is a core value of your faith life that comes to mind after learning about restorative justice? . . . Mercy? Hope? Redemption? Movement toward forgiveness? What is the connection between that value and addressing harm?

Chapter 2

When We Experience Harm

There is so much division in our world today. The news reminds us of how opposing groups clash with one another, human dignity is violated, and competition, rather than collaboration, is the name of the game. On a personal level, perhaps, we never feel more divided than when we have been hurt by someone. The injury violates our sense of connection and trust. It is all too easy today to allow these divisions to go unamended, simply casting someone off when we feel wronged by him or her. Such casting off can take many different forms: holding a grudge, disconnecting on social media, ending a relationship, isolation through imprisonment, or, in the most extreme cases, execution.

But Jesus shows us another way of responding to harm and violence. Jesus' words and actions reflect the biblical concept of shalom, a vision of wholeness, unity, and integrity that God desires for all creation. This is made manifest in how he performs miracles of healing, drives out evil spirits, and teaches us to love our enemies. These teachings and examples are central to our call to restorative justice. When we suffer because of crime, injustice, or everyday interactions, we look to Jesus' example in mending the brokenness and, where possible, making things right again.

Think back on a time when you felt wronged by someone. Maybe the hurt resulted from a miscommunication or maybe it was a deliberate act intended to cause emotional or physical pain. This person may have been a stranger, an acquaintance, a relative, or someone with whom you felt especially close. How did you feel when this incident happened? Disappointed, hurt, angry, betrayed, saddened, afraid? Probably the impact was emotional, but maybe also material, physical, or spiritual. What transpired as a result of that interaction?

Restorative practices mentioned in chapter 1 allow opportunities to address these various consequences and can repair the harm done, to the greatest extent possible. Our criminal justice system teaches that punishment for a crime holds a perpetrator accountable, but punishment alone cannot repair the actual damage caused. It can be helpful to think about what this looks like in a specific instance.

Jane's Story

Jane arrived home from work to find her house broken into and valuables missing, including a strand of pearls she had inherited from her grandmother. Jane was heartbroken about the pearls and angry about the damage to her house. Worse yet, she felt unsafe in her own home. For days she lived in constant fear of it happening again. Her fear turned to shock when police revealed that the person who had broken into her house was her own neighbor, a teenage girl Jane had known for years. She felt especially betrayed remembering the birthday parties they had celebrated together and the ways Jane had looked out for the young woman as she was growing up.[1]

The Many Impacts of Harm

Like many people harmed by a crime, Jane felt the aftereffects of this event in more ways than one. One of the reasons that restorative practices are so powerful is because they can play an important role in the process of trauma healing. In *Redemption and Restoration*, Timothy Wolfe describes the various ways that trauma can impact someone's life if it goes unaddressed: "The experience of being victimized by crime, whether it be a minor or major offense, can be traumatizing and can produce long-term effects ranging from fear, immobilizing anxiety, anger, and financial losses, to a sense of loss of control, withdrawal, and alienation. With attention focused on pursuing prosecution and punishing the criminal, victims can often feel forgotten and marginalized."[2] Prolonged experience of such marginalization can result in depression or other forms of mental illness, loss of faith, or self-destructive behaviors such as drug or alcohol abuse. These are all potential outcomes when trauma is unhealed and manifested internally. In other cases, unhealed hurt can cause someone to act out in ways that harm others. In many cases, someone who commits a crime was first a victim of violence themselves.[3]

The aftermath of such an experience can vary dramatically depending on the person and the nature of the crime. In some cases, the healing process is made especially difficult when a person's community is not prepared to support them in their healing process. In Catholic Mobilizing Network's work to end the death penalty, the testimonies of families who have lost loved ones illustrate these effects. Not only were family members suffering immeasurable pain and unable to have a voice in the criminal justice proceedings, some no longer felt welcome in their own faith communities. Fellow parishioners were unprepared or unable to support families after a tragic loss and distanced themselves. Yet, when an individual is harmed, entire communities are affected. All need support and healing. As God commands, we are called to love God and our neighbor as ourselves (Matt 22:36-40). In chapter 4, we will explore more deeply the role of communities in restorative justice.

A Catholic Family's Journey
In 2010, Kate and Deacon Andy Grosmaire learned that their daughter Ann had been shot by her fiancé, Conor. Moved by their Catholic faith to forgive Conor, and dissatisfied by the criminal justice process, the Grosmaires, along with Conor's parents, Michael and Julie McBride, fought to address the crime in a way that allowed their voices to be heard. At an event on November 5, 2018, Kate and Deacon Andy told their personal story of restorative justice. You can watch their talk at: www.catholicsmobilizing .org/rj-reader-guide

Opportunities for Healing

There are a number of things that can contribute to healing after an instance of harm including prayer, support from loved ones, spiritual direction, counseling, and artistic expression. Taking part in a restorative justice process can be especially transformative because it gives victims an opportunity to tell their story, have their questions answered, and receive assurances that the perpetrators are remorseful and will attempt to change their behavior. It also allows the offender to hear and understand better the impact of their actions and make amends. Each of these contributes to healing for the person(s) harmed, enabling them to move forward in a positive way, no longer crippled by the event they experienced.

Pope Francis affirms this vision of restorative justice in relation to the death penalty when he says, "The Lord has gradually taught his people that there is a necessary asymmetry between crime and punishment, that one cannot apply the remedy: an eye for an eye or a tooth for a broken tooth, by breaking that of another. Justice is to be rendered to the victim not by executing the aggressor."[4] Likewise, simply incarcerating an offender does not heal a victim's pain.

Revisiting Jane's story earlier in the chapter, Jane most wanted to restore her sense of safety. She also wished for her young neighbor to understand the impact of her actions. She wanted the damage to her home and belongings repaired, but Jane also knew that a prison sentence would interfere with future employment, school, and other opportunities for the teen. Because she knew this young woman and her family so well, Jane especially wanted to have a say in the process and what would happen next for her.

Restorative Justice Handout
CMN's one-page handout gives an introductory overview of restorative justice and ways practices can be applied in various settings. Download and print copies to complement an educational workshop or spread the word about restorative justice with others in your community. To view and download, visit: www.catholicsmobilizing.org/rj -reader-guide

Family, Community, and Participation

The principles of Catholic social teaching remind us that each of us has been bestowed a God-given dignity. That dignity is exercised in relationships, namely, in the core interconnectedness of family, our local and global communities, and the social interactions and civic life we participate in. It is through relationships that the love of Christ is brought to life. The United States Conference of Catholic Bishops states: "The principle of participation is especially important for victims of crime. Sometimes victims are 'used' by the criminal justice system or political interests. As the prosecution builds a case, the victim's hurt and loss can be seen as a tool to obtain convictions and tough sentences. But the victim's need to be heard and to be healed are not really addressed."[5] In traditional justice, the court determines what "justice" should be. In restorative justice, the victim plays a central role in determining what justice should look like.

As you have read, one restorative practice that allows the person(s) harmed to participate fully in the process is victim-offender dialogue. In some cases, like Jane's, this dialogue can influence the outcome of the sentence. If this is not possible, some jurisdictions invite victims to provide an impact statement. Unfortunately, in many cases, victims are not even kept informed about the status of their case, or if/when the perpetrator is released from prison. Restorative approaches to harm offer victims greater opportunities to participate in the process and its outcome.

Restorative Justice Ministry: San Francisco
In the Archdiocese of San Francisco, Julio Escobar leads "A Ministry of Presence." Through this ministry, those who have lost loved ones to homicide support one another on

their healing journey. Together they memorialize the location where their loved one died and are present with others who have experienced similar loss and grief. When family members feel ready, they visit with individuals in juvenile hall to share their stories. These encounters offer an opportunity for those responsible for crimes to think differently about the harms they committed and consider the impacts of their actions. They also allow victims to share the stories of their loved ones in ways that may prevent future violence. Watch the video at: www.catholicsmobilizing.org/rj-reader -guide

Again, considering the example of Jane's story, through a restorative dialogue, Jane, the young woman, and her parents came together with a trained facilitator to discuss the break-in. Jane described her sadness, fear, and anger. In response, the young woman expressed guilt, shame, and remorse. Through the dialogue, they agreed that the young woman would pay for the damages and return what she had stolen. Together, the group agreed to ensure that the young woman would receive treatment for the drug problem that led her to burgle Jane's house.

What about Forgiveness?

You may have noticed that in Jane's story we didn't hear about forgiveness. Perhaps this was surprising? Sometimes people think of apology and forgiveness as the central point or "end goal" of restorative justice. Indeed, restorative dialogues can open up the possibility for reconciliation to take place, but forgiveness is not a requirement of restorative practices. That said, as Christians, the call to forgive others compels us to practice restorative justice whenever possible, which is evidenced in the Grosmaires' story earlier in the chapter. As Trudy Conway describes in *Redemption and Restoration*, "The Catholic tradition, in both its Scriptures and practices, places great emphasis on forgiveness—both the acts of forgiving and being forgiven. Christ calls all Christians to forgive seventy times seven without end and to realize that our wrongs will be forgiven as we forgive those who have wronged us."[6]

Even if spoken apology and forgiveness do not take place at the time of the meeting, restorative justice can play an important role in the victim's healing journey that may eventually lead to forgiveness. Forgiving others can release feelings of destructive anger for both sides. It may not eliminate all negative emotions, but it can dramatically reduce them. In addition to changing how we feel, forgiveness also changes how we act. Desmond Tutu says that "forgiving means abandoning your right to pay back the perpetrator in his own coin."[7] In other words, in forgiving, the person harmed no longer wishes to repay suffering with further suffering and is freed of feelings of vengeance. When we forgive others, we acknowledge that we, too, have hurt others. In this way, we recognize our common humanity and our common dignity.

The primary goal of restorative justice is to restore the person(s) harmed to wholeness to the greatest extent possible. This involves answering questions that help to reestablish a sense of safety, repairing damages, and making amends through restitution or other activities that contribute to healing relationships among the victim, the offender, and the wider community. A key component of this restoration is that the person who committed the harm takes responsibility. In the next chapter, we will consider the importance of accountability in allowing all those involved to move forward.

Prayer

Dear Lord, we pray for victims of violence and their families, that they may experience our love and support and find comfort in your compassion and loving embrace. We hold in prayer all the times that we have experienced harm in any form. Grant us the courage to seek out restorative encounters to bring about your vision of healing and unity that we, your people, may no longer be divided by our brokenness. Help us practice forgiveness in the small things, so we may embody your spirit of healing and restoration in all things.

Reflection Questions:

1. Is there an instance from your own life in which you were harmed and are in need of healing? What do you feel you need from the person(s) who caused that harm in order to make things right again?

2. Do you know someone who has been impacted by crime and may be in need of support? Consider the various ways the incident may have damaged relationships, safety, or the day-to-day life of this person. What could you do to support this person on their healing journey?

3. How does your community attend to the needs of victims of crime? Does your local jurisdiction allow victims to have a say in litigation surrounding their crime, or allow access to information about the proceedings? Does your parish or diocese offer spaces for victims of crime to come together for support?

Chapter 3

When We Cause Harm

In ideal circumstances, a restorative justice process, involves victims, offenders, and communities, although it is important to acknowledge that this is not always possible. This may be because there are extenuating circumstances, parties are not ready or willing to meet, or coming together would have the potential to be retraumatizing for those involved. Such processes should always be voluntary. Especially when grave harm has occurred, there is extensive preparation that happens individually before a direct encounter takes place. With all of this in mind, the previous chapter focused on the role of the victim, because their involvement is a large part of what sets restorative justice apart from traditional criminal justice.

As we move forward to consider the role of the person who caused harm, it is important to remember that every person is more than the worst thing they have ever suffered or done. Sometimes using the language of "victim" and "offender" is used because it is the language that people are most familiar with, but it is limiting—implying that this label represents a person's entire being. Throughout this book, we seek to describe the roles of those involved in restorative justice practices in a variety of ways. As you talk with others about restorative justice or issues of criminal justice, you are encouraged to reflect upon language that honors human dignity of all. In reading this chapter, you will also come to see the ways in which these roles are interrelated.

When we think about someone who is labeled an "offender," some people reading this book might think to themselves, "No one in my life has committed a crime." Others may think of a loved one who is currently or formerly incarcerated. Regardless of how we identify with this role in relation to criminal justice, we all must come face-to-face with one question: "In my lifetime, have I ever done or said something that has hurt someone else?" As fully human beings, and therefore sinners, when we are honest with ourselves, we know that the answer to this question is always "yes." We may not intend to cause harm and don't always realize it when we do, but a key aspect of restorative justice is taking responsibility for our actions. We can only expect this of others if we are willing to do so ourselves.

Perhaps as you read this, there is a particular instance that comes to mind. Maybe the harm seemed small, like putting your own interests above someone else's needs or feeding into gossip. Or it may have been more significant, bullying someone physically or emotionally, telling a lie that damaged someone's well-being, or taking something that wasn't yours. Perhaps it was an action severe enough that broke a law and involved the criminal justice system.

As you recall this event, what happened afterward? Did you admit what you had done . . . to yourself, the person you harmed, or others? Did you feel remorse? Did you ever have the opportunity to express that remorse to those affected or do anything to help make it right again? What happened as a result? As you read this chapter, hold this instance and these questions with grace. You will have the opportunity to return to them through Scripture, stories, and prayer.

Lessons from Scripture on Accountability

First, we'll turn to the Bible. In *Redemption and Restoration*, Richard Buck looks to the book of Leviticus and its insight about how different kinds of wrongdoing are to be addressed. Too often, our society refers to sections of Hebrew Scripture as justification for harsh punishment: death, for example, as payback for worshiping idols or for failure to honor the Sabbath. However, a closer look will show that these punishments are not meant as revenge but as part of a purification process. These responses to sin were intended to lead the sinner to atonement through self-sacrifice and repentance. More severe punishments were imposed when someone intentionally acted in a way that rejected his or her community and relationship with God, but even then, repentance was still possible. After all, *teshuvah*, the Hebrew word for "repentance," literally means "return."

This is very different from modern culture, where we are not generally encouraged to admit when we've done something wrong. Either we are afraid of the repercussions, or we are simply embarrassed. Pride too often gets in the way of honesty, humility, and willingness to be vulnerable with one another. Perhaps nowhere is this more evident than in our legal system. When someone is apprehended for a crime, they are frequently advised not to say anything because it could be used against them. Even when learning to drive, instructors tell students never to admit fault for a car accident. This is a small example of the way our culture has reinforced avoiding accountability. Instead of being open and taking responsibility for our actions, we blame others and look for technicalities that will get us "off the hook."

In a restorative approach, accountability is achieved when a person takes responsibility and makes amends for their actions. The book of Ezekiel says, "And though I say to the wicked that they shall die, if they turn away from sin and do what is just and right—returning pledges, restoring stolen goods, walking by statutes that bring life, doing nothing wrong—they shall surely live; they shall not die. None of the sins they committed shall be remembered against them. If they do what is right and just, they shall surely live" (Ezek 33:14-16).

In our retributive legal system, "justice" is served through the assigning of punishment, which usually takes the form of incarceration. In some ways, the current prison system in which individuals are isolated in cells was intended to model a monastic way of life. The idea was that a person's behaviors would change after a period of time reflecting on their actions. This is where the term "penitentiary" came from. But we now know that this time of being removed from society often has consequences that are more detrimental than reformative. Parents are separated from their children, wage-earners cannot support their family's finances, and various aspects of mental, physical, and spiritual health often go unattended. While some correctional facilities have education and job training programs, attempts to reenter the workforce with a criminal record make it extremely challenging to become employed after release.

In *Redemption and Restoration*, Richard Buck points out that prisons, in which isolation serves as punishment for long periods of time, are not a part of the biblical justice system. In Scripture, the few references to imprisonment are brief and highly circumstantial. Buck says, "The lack of punitive incarceration clearly shows that in the view of Jewish law, putting criminals in prison for long periods of time does not satisfy the demands of justice for either the offender or the victim."[1]

Frequently, people cite the "eye for an eye" passage (Lev 24:17, 19-20) as justification for retribution, but in truth, this passage was intended to limit revenge and call for restitution. For severe offenses such as killing, the Old Testament describes fleeing to a city of refuge. Richard Buck explains, "the purpose of these cities was not to punish through isolation, but rather to provide for the killer a safe and easily accessible place to reflect on what had been done and embark on a process of *teshuva*, leading, ultimately, to atonement."[2] Here, we can see that even when offenders were sent into exile, they were still part of a community. It is important that even when punishment is warranted, it includes opportunities for connection, redemption, and re-integration into society.

Prayer Vigil for an Execution

The recent revision to the Catechism states that "there is an increasing awareness that the dignity of the person is not lost even after the commission of very serious crimes. In addition, a new understanding has emerged of the significance of penal sanctions imposed by the state. Lastly, more effective systems of detention have been developed, which ensure the due protection of citizens but, at the same time, do not definitively deprive the guilty of the possibility of redemption. Consequently, the Church teaches, in the light of the Gospel, that 'the death penalty is inadmissible because it is an attack on the inviolability and dignity of the person,' and she works with determination for its abolition worldwide."[3] Church teaching makes it clear that even if incarceration is needed for community safety, it should not be without the oppor-

tunity for transformation and hope. This vigil invites us
to prayerfully honor the lives and dignity of those facing
imminent execution and all those who are incarcerated.
To download the vigil, visit: www.catholicsmobilizing.org
/rj-reader-guide

Tony's Story

By the time Tony Hicks was fourteen, he had been
through a lot. His father abandoned him at a young age
and he was angry enough to run away from home. When he
did, he brought his grandfather's gun with him, which he
had planned to sell as a way to support himself. On a winter
night in 1995, Tony and his friends had a plan. They would
order a pizza, give a fake address, and attempt to rob the
confused delivery person. Tariq Khamisa was completing his
last delivery of the night and as he looked for the apartment
a nearby teen demanded the pizzas. Another young person
stood nearby with a gun. Tariq realized what was about to
happen, tossed the pizzas in his car, and attempted to drive
away, but was killed by Tony's only shot. Because California
had recently passed its "tough on crime" bill, Tony was tried
as an adult and given a far longer sentence than if he had
been tried as a juvenile.

Many members of the community called for retribution,
but this bothered Azim, Tariq's father, who was a devout
Muslim. Rather than punishment, Azim was more interested
in what led to such a tragic event. How could three young
people do such a horrible thing? Azim understood that there
are root causes of violence that must be addressed in order
to prevent lives from being lost. Together, Azim, Ples (Tony's
grandfather), and, eventually, Tony himself worked together
to start a foundation that educates young people about the

impacts of violence. Not only did this work transform the lives of other young people, but it also helped Tony to take responsibility for his actions and all three to find healing.[4]

Rights and Responsibilities

The creation story declares that every person is made in the image and likeness of God. Inherent in the dignity that God bestows on each person are both rights and responsibilities. We have a right to life itself and rights to basic human needs that make life livable, such as food, housing, healthcare, education, and safety. The flip side of rights are responsibilities. Each person has certain responsibilities toward other persons, society, and the common good. Catholic social teaching contends that to be human is to experience not only certain rights but also obligations toward people and the community.

As Susan Sharpe, restorative justice advisor at University of Notre Dame, describes:

> Restorative justice recognizes that rights and responsibilities are interwoven, that living justly in community requires being accountable for how our choices affect other people. Thus, someone who has caused harm to another has a primary obligation to help repair it and may be the only one who can provide what is needed (such as an explanation of why they made the choice they did). Yet restorative justice recognizes that some needs are best met by people other than the one responsible (such as accompaniment or counseling to help restore a sense of safety), and that the common good depends on community members' sharing responsibility for ensuring that justice needs are met.[5]

It is easy to think that when a crime happens, only the person who committed the offense is responsible for making it right. Though, when all those impacted have a voice in the process, it becomes more apparent that creative and collaborative solutions can meaningfully contribute to repair.

Meeting Needs and Taking Responsibility

In many cases, if someone causes harm, in one way or another his or her basic needs were not being met. Perhaps there was a material need for money or food, although often actions are motivated by deeper needs for a sense of protection, identity, inclusion, or power. In addition, someone may be acting out of hurt, because her or his own dignity or rights were violated. Young people are especially sensitive to the effects of these adverse experiences, but too frequently they do not have the means or support to respond in a healthy way.

This is why restorative practices can be especially effective in schools. Using restorative dialogue to address student misconduct includes not only students and administration, but also teachers, parents, and friends, so that everyone can be a part of determining an appropriate response to the problem and assuring that the students' needs are being met both inside and outside of school. More and more schools are also using circles to share stories and process events, helping to build stronger bonds and stop violence before it starts.

However, adverse experiences are not only a concern for youth. Many times, adults who are convicted of a crime have a history of traumatic experiences themselves, whether as victims of abuse or neglect, or ongoing stressors of racial discrimination or living in poverty. In order for restorative justice to be successful, the person who committed the harm must take responsibility, be accountable for their actions, and take steps to make things right. In addition, all members of society have a responsibility to make basic human rights accessible in order to prevent violence and reduce recidivism.

Bridges to Life Restorative Justice Program
Bridges to Life, an in-prison restorative justice program based in Texas, combines restorative dialogue between incarcerated individuals and victims of similar crimes with life-skills training and spiritual support to inspire change that brings healing and reduces recidivism. To watch a video about how it works, visit: www.catholicsmobilizing .org/rj-reader-guide

Rethinking Incarceration

Many of the examples we have considered involve cases of violent crime. However, a vast number of individuals in prison are there because of nonviolent crimes such as possession of illegal drugs. Throughout the 1970s, '80s, and '90s drug laws became more and more punitive, based on the theory that harsh punishments would deter drug related activity. The so-called "war on drugs" created mandatory minimum sentencing that required specific, often long prison sentences for nonviolent drug charges regardless of a person's past experiences or specific needs. Unlike than treatment and rehabilitative services to address addiction, time in prison often further marginalizes someone who is already struggling.

In addition, some policing practices purposefully target African American and Hispanic individuals and communities in order to meet quotas for arrests. For example, a study in North Carolina documented that black drivers were far more likely to be stopped, searched, and, therefore, arrested than white drivers.[6] Timothy Wolfe points out in *Redemption and Restoration*, "We also know that police in large cities (e.g., NYC) and smaller towns (e.g., Ferguson, MO) across the country are more likely to stop and frisk young minority males than any other demographic group."[7] As a result, two-thirds of people in prison for drug offenses are people of color, even though whites and minorities have similar rates of drug use.[8] To address these problems, some communities have created restorative drug courts that bring families and support people together to create a plan for addressing addiction in the life of their loved one. Continued work is also needed, however, to combat racial bias in policing and many restorative justice organizations make this an element of their work.

A Native American Tribe Is Using Traditional Culture to Fight Addiction

Some people turn to drug use because they feel disconnected from their family, community, or culture. A community in Maine is using restorative circles to rebuild relationships and reclaim cultural identity in ways that are fighting the opioid epidemic. To watch the video, visit: www.catholicsmobilizing.org/rj-reader-guide

There are countless changes needed throughout society to reduce violence and honor human dignity for all those who are touched by the criminal justice system. Creating more opportunities for restorative practices can go a long way in transforming the lives of those who cause harm. We recall the words of Richard Rohr, OFM, who says, "If we do not transform our pain, we will most assuredly transmit it."[9] And so, let us consider ways to respond to Pope Francis's call when he spoke at Curran-Fromhold Correctional Facility in Philadelphia during his historic visit to the United States in 2015: "Let us heal that pain and welcome every person who has committed offenses, who admits their failures, is repentant and truly wants to make reparation, thus contributing to the building of a new order where justice and peace shine forth."[10]

Prayer

Lord, I am a broken person. I have sinned, against you and against others. My actions have consequences beyond what I can fully know, and beyond what I may feel able to admit in this moment. Help me to take responsibility for my actions. As I recall the past and look to the future, give me the courage to seek forgiveness from those I have harmed. When confronted with the pain I have caused others, help me to listen with humility and do what I can to make it right again. In my brokenness, give me courage to encounter others who have caused harm with compassion and to seek justice and mercy in the path to redemption.

Reflection Questions:

1. At the beginning of this chapter you were invited to reflect on a time that you caused harm to someone else. When you think back on that situation or another one, what could be done to make it right?

2. Next time you're watching the news, listen for information about the life of the person who committed the crime. What basic rights and needs were not met in their lives? How might their own human dignity have been violated? What changes may have interrupted the cycles of violence?

3. When Pope Francis visited Curran-Fromhold Correctional Facility he brought a message of hope and redemption. How can you be a messenger of hope to someone who is responsible for causing harm?

Chapter 4

When We Consider Community, Systems, and Structures

So far, we have spent time considering the experiences of those who directly suffer from or are responsible for crime. Furthermore, we know that we have all been hurt and caused hurt to others. In each instance, there were also people indirectly impacted by the harm.

The three parties that restorative justice prioritizes are often referred to as victims, offenders, and communities. In a particular restorative justice process, community members might include family members, friends, neighbors, colleagues, or volunteers. When we zoom out and remember that we are all integrally connected, we also see that the systems and structures at play in our everyday lives are a part of this web of relationships. Even if you don't feel directly impacted by crime or incarceration, how is our broken criminal justice system affecting your community? Perhaps an even more challenging question—if everything is connected, do you and I contribute to its brokenness?

In this chapter, we will consider the ways in which we are all responsible for one another and explore opportunities for reconciliation within our immediate communities as it relates to harm and criminal justice. More broadly, we will examine the systems and structures—that we knowingly or unknowingly participate in—that violate God's vision for unity and communion with one another.

My Community

If someone you know has suffered through a difficult time, you probably remember suffering vicariously, experiencing sorrow and pain yourself. If someone you love was responsible for causing harm, you may have experienced a sense of shame and wondered if something you had done contributed to his or her actions. When a restorative dialogue takes place, these are the reasons why community members, family, friends, neighbors, or colleagues are invited to be a part of the process, to offer support, have their own questions answered, and contribute to an agreement plan for restoration.

Even those with more distant connections to the incident have questions and concerns that, often, the traditional criminal justice system doesn't address. In *Redemption and Restoration*, Trudy Conway remembers a crime in her town covered by local media. Members of the town were asking: "How are interactions with the prosecution team affecting victims? Does the judge and the offender understand the depth of suffering of the victims? Can a long prison term address the wrongs done to victims' families? What effect will imprisonment in a different state have on the young children of the offender? Does the offender understand the impact of this crime on our entire community? How can we prevent others from becoming victims of such a crime?"[1] Restorative justice calls upon communities to not only support those directly impacted, but also consider their own role in the harm itself, what contributed to causing it, and how to make things right. In this section, we will explore our communal role in transforming the larger criminal justice system.

One Human Family

Violence and harm have rippling effects. Beyond that, as Catholics we believe the whole human family is connected in a web of relationships. Pope Francis writes about this interconnectedness in *Laudato Si'*. He says, "Since everything is closely interrelated, and today's problems call for a vision capable of taking into account every aspect of the global crisis, I suggest that we now consider some elements of an *integral ecology*, one which clearly respects its human and social dimensions."[2]

This is closely connected to the concept of *ubuntu*, a Swahili word frequently translated as "I am because we are." *Ubuntu* holds particular significance to restorative justice because of the Truth and Reconciliation Commission processes that took place in South Africa. In 1948, a white nationalist government enforced a system of racial segregation called apartheid. For the next fifty years nonwhite South Africans were subjected to extreme oppression and violence. In 1994, apartheid ended and a democratic government was established. Recognizing that grave offenses had been committed, the only way to move forward was to be fully truthful about the events of the past; a nongovernmental commission created opportunities for those who had lost loved ones to share their stories, for those who had committed violence to take ownership, and for all members of society to bear witness and contribute to finding a new way forward. Anglican Archbishop Desmond Tutu, who had opposed and fought against apartheid, was appointed as head of the commission.

In *No Future without Forgiveness,* Tutu reflects upon his experience. He explains *ubuntu* this way:

> My humanity is caught up, is inextricably bound up, in yours. . . . A person with ubuntu is open and available to others, affirming of others, does not feel threatened that others are able and good, for he or she has a proper self-assurance that comes from knowing that he or she belongs in a greater whole and is diminished when others are humiliated or diminished, when others are tortured or oppressed, or treated as if they were less than who they are.[3]

When we openly listen to and share stories about our personal experiences, we build empathy for one another, see what we share in common, and recognize one another's God-given dignity. Strong communities, parishes, and organizations have means of building relationships by sharing experiences. This in turn, enables us to support one another in times of difficulty, harm, and conflict. Restorative practices create opportunities for such encounter to take place.

Solidarity and Subsidiarity

Ubuntu has a close connection with concepts of solidarity and subsidiarity in Catholic social tradition. The United States Conference of Catholic Bishops describes solidarity this way: "We are one human family whatever our national, racial, ethnic, economic, and ideological differences. We are our brothers' and sisters' keepers, wherever they may be. Loving our neighbor has global dimensions in a shrinking world."[4] In other words, when one of us suffers, we all suffer together. Likewise, if we are interconnected so that the consequences of crime affect us all, then we are all responsible for one another too. In *Redemption and Restoration,* William

Collinge explains: "Subsidiarity calls on us to strengthen families and local communities and deal with social problems first on those levels, while recognizing that larger, systemic approaches may also be needed."[5]

Now that we've learned about restorative practices such as circles and victim-offender dialogue, we can see how this teaching is lived out through individual practices. How can the sacraments help us along the journey?

> **Pathways to Restoration Webpage**
> Catholic Mobilizing Network's *Pathways to Restoration* offers stories to spark imagination, resources for learning and discerning next steps, and tools for action and change. Included are examples of ways that restorative circles and dialogue are used in various communities. This dynamic online toolkit offers individuals and communities an easy place to start in the journey to becoming agents of restoration. You can access this page through: www.catholicsmobilizing.org/rj-reader-guide

The Sacraments and Restoration

In the Catholic tradition, the sacraments teach us valuable lessons about healing relationships with God and others. In baptism Christians "recognize this pattern of living—suffering, death, and resurrection—and see this pattern as a way of imitating and conforming themselves to Christ in the actions of their daily lives."[11] The celebration of the Eucharist is a weekly (or daily) reminder of this cycle, too. Perhaps most applicable to the conversation on restorative justice is the sacrament of reconciliation. We often think of penance only in our sins against God, but it is also intended to serve as "reconciliation with our brethren and sisters who remain harmed by our sins."[12] Each of the church's three penitential rites includes elements that focus on social sin such as racism. This penance prepares our hearts and spirits for the forgiveness, reconciliation, and restorative justice that is needed in our communities.

Participating in the sacrament of reconciliation can be very challenging; it is never easy to let go of our pride, admit our faults, ask for forgiveness, and commit to acts of prayer and service that bring absolution. But we are comforted in knowing that we humbly bring ourselves to an ever loving and forgiving God. Because of this, many of us find the more frequently we enter into this sacrament, the easier it becomes. Likewise, the more we make a habit of bringing the practices of confession and reconciliation into relationships with those around us, the easier it becomes. As mentioned before, small changes can go a long way in our day-to-day interactions. Because we have all been touched by the brokenness of the criminal justice system in one way or another, it is our shared responsibility to transform it. As you will read in the following sections, we all share the burden of its brokenness. The sacraments prepare our hearts, minds, and spirits to engage with our communities and systems—the world around us—in more healing ways.

The Costs of Incarceration

Incarceration rates in the United States are higher than they've ever been, with one in every 110 adults behind bars.[6] Though it contains only 5 percent of the world's population, the United States houses more than 20 percent of the world's prison population.[7] This has profound implications for our economy. Based on a 2012 report, approximately $274 billion, or $870 per capita, in tax dollars are spent each year to fund federal, state, and local jails and prisons along with courts and offices overseeing parole and probation.[8] It is also important to remember there are many private companies that provide services and resources within the prison system and communities who rely upon prisons as major sources of employment. Some have referred to this as a "prison industrial complex," in which entire economies depend upon crime and punishment to survive or profit.

These economic costs are staggering, but there are human costs as well. The bonds of family are sacred and essential to creating a world in which every person can thrive and share the love of Christ. If one in every 110 adults is in prison, then that many people are disconnected from their spouses, parents, children, and siblings. As Christians who value the integrity of family, we know this separation has detrimental consequences for young people and adults alike, from absence of role models and support people to increased stressors that result from limited income. As one human family, our brothers and sisters are suffering. The letter to the Hebrews reminds us how we are called to respond as community: "Let mutual love continue. Do not neglect to show hospitality to strangers, for by doing that some have entertained angels without knowing it. Remember those who are in prison, as though you were in prison with them; those who are being tortured, as though you yourselves were being tortured" (Heb 13:1-3).

The Sin of Racism

Restorative practices can play a critical role in reducing prison populations. From victim-offender dialogues that create alternatives to prison time, to circles of support for trauma healing, across the country, such community-based solutions are combating disproportionate rates of incarceration among people of color. Additionally, when we consider issues of racism through a lens of restorative justice, we may start to understand our nation's history and present-day challenges differently.

In November of 2018, the United States Conference of Catholic Bishops released a pastoral letter against racism called *Open Wide Our Hearts: The Enduring Call to Love.* The letter summarizes the many ways that Native Americans, African Americans, and Hispanics have been harmed throughout our nation's history and the ways racism is institutionalized within political and cultural structures. In this section, we take a specific look at the treatment of people of African descent in the US criminal justice system.

European settlers committed terrible acts of violence against African peoples by uprooting them from their homes and families, forcing them into slavery, and subjecting them to beating, killing, rape, and countless other forms of violent oppression. In today's era we may think to ourselves, "Yes, that was terrible, but I am not one of those settlers," or "What does that have to do with the criminal justice system today?"

Though the Thirteenth Amendment[9] abolished slavery in 1865, an exception was allowed for it in the case of punishment for a crime. In the years that followed, those in power sought to criminalize the behavior of African Americans. In *The New Jim Crow*,[10] Michelle Alexander breaks down this history to reveal how our criminal justice system's policies and practices still serve to marginalize and dehumanize people of color. In addition, the historical harms of slavery and lynching are still felt in the lives of many today. The changes that we make in our criminal justice system, communities, and daily interactions that prioritize the dignity, rights, and needs of individuals of color are deliberate steps toward repairing the harms committed against our brothers and sisters.

TED Talk: We Need to Talk about an Injustice
In 2018, Bryan Stevenson with Equal Justice Initiative opened the Legacy Museum: From Enslavement to Mass Incarceration and The National Memorial for Peace and Justice to commemorate the lives of those enslaved and lynched in America. These memorials compel us to encounter and come to terms with the injuries of our country's past, to understand their impact in the present, and to consider how we can play a role in building a better future. In this video, Bryan Stevenson goes into more depth about the relationship between race, the criminal justice system, and beyond. To watch the talk, visit: www.catholics mobilizing.org/rj-reader-guide

Finding Solutions in Our Communities

The scope of problems in our criminal justice system may feel discouraging, perhaps even overwhelming. Where do we start? Is there a way out of this darkness? Those who contributed to the early development of restorative practices asked themselves the same questions. They looked at the criminal justice system and thought, "There must be a better way."

Circles can be a powerful tool for building community in addition to addressing specific instances of harm. When used informally to explore a topic of interest, get to know one another, or share in gratitude and celebration, they create opportunities to more deeply connect with one another. By going around in the order of seating and using a talking piece to signal the speaker, we are better able to listen deeply rather than planning what we will say next. This intentional presence creates a space to share stories and reflections from personal experience that often get drowned out in the day-to-day hustle and bustle of life. Ultimately, through this sharing and presence, we can build and strengthen bonds that honor our common humanity. Then, even when we disagree with one another, we recognize our shared God-given dignity, and we may be less likely to cause one another harm in the future. In other words, by building community, restorative practices can respond to harm, but also help to prevent it. The more we practice this healing way of interacting with one another, the more ready we will be to bring it to the communities, structures, and systems around us.

Prayer

The cause for sainthood of Chief Nicholas Black Elk was opened in 2017. A Lakota man, he became Catholic and was an active catechist "melding his Lakota culture into his Christian life."[13] In this passage, he describes the significance of the circle in the lives of Native peoples. You are invited to pray about the spirit and significance of circles as they are used in restorative practices and reflect our common unity with one another and the earth.

> You have noticed that everything an Indian does is in a circle, and that is because the Power of the World always works in circles, and everything tries to be round. In the old days . . . all our power came to us from the sacred hoop of the nation, and so long as the hoop was unbroken, the people flourished. . . . Everything the power of the world does is done in a circle. The sky is round, and I have heard that the earth is round like a ball, and so are all the stars. The wind, in its greatest power, whirls. Birds make their nests in circles, for theirs is the same religion as ours. The sun comes forth and goes down again in a circle. The moon does the same, and both are round. Even

the seasons form a great circle in their changing, and always come back again to where they were. The life of a man is a circle from childhood to childhood, and so it is in everything where power moves. Our teepees were round like the nests of birds, and these were always set in a circle, the nation's hoop, a nest of many nests, where the Great Spirit meant for us to hatch our children.[14]

Reflection Questions:

1. Consider the Beatitudes in Matthew 5:3-12 in terms of restorative justice and the coming kingdom of God. Now, think about them as actual ways of living that will bring restoration and peace. How can the Beatitudes help to guide you in your communal response to violence and harm?

2. It is proven that "tough on crime" and "war on drugs" tactics do not deter illegal activity, but instead increase incarceration rates. If these approaches are ineffective, why do you think they are still revered in American culture?

3. Community members are invited to be a part of restorative dialogues following an incident of harm. Circles can be used to build community among people who are proximate to one another. What do you see as the relationship between strengthening ties and responding to harm?

Chapter 5

When We Become Agents of Restoration

[F]rom now on we regard no one according to the flesh; even if we once knew Christ according to the flesh, yet now we know him so no longer. So whoever is in Christ is a new creation: the old things have passed away; behold, new things have come. And all this is from God, who has reconciled us to himself through Christ and given us the ministry of reconciliation, namely, God was reconciling the world to himself in Christ, not counting their trespasses against them and entrusting to us the message of reconciliation. (2 Cor 5:15-19)

Jesus not only modeled how to live restoratively, but his death and resurrection, in atonement for our sins, was the ultimate act of restorative justice. This redemption and promise of salvation implores us to be ministers of reconciliation. Ultimate reconciliation between people is not always possible, but, as with forgiveness, we can see reconciliation as a journey. Restorative justice offers a path to follow on that journey, and its practices can help guide our steps.

There are so many areas of our world that cry out for reconciliation, and calls to transform our broken criminal justice system are loud. The earlier chapters offered insights into a different way of thinking about crime and harm, other than the punitive approaches that our traditional criminal justice system espouses.

Through the lens of our Catholic faith and the wisdom of other spiritual traditions throughout the world, we see a restorative way that upholds human dignity and fosters a culture of life by healing people and relationships. In our current society, that better way feels distant, perhaps even impossible. How can we ever achieve it? It won't be easy, and it won't be quick, but thus is the work of building the kingdom of God. As Trudy Conway tells us in *Redemption and Restoration*, "Restorative justice is thus future-oriented. . . . Such a shift in response to crime and criminal justice leads to shaping practices that bring persons and society to actively and responsibly work to right the wrongs done to persons by a crime. It also leads to recognizing the role of community in actively responding to crime."[1]

We have learned that harm and suffering have ripple effects. The good news is, healing can have ripple effects too. Janine Geske's work is a wonderful example of this. While serving as a judge on the Supreme Court for the state of Wisconsin, she heard about restorative justice. She was skeptical at first, but decided it was worth learning more. Upon observing circles and victim-offender dialogues, she was moved to start facilitating circles in the Green Bay prisons. A devout Catholic who was also a professor at Marquette University, she created an institute to educate students and others about restorative justice. Justice Geske continues to write and speak about the transformative power of restorative justice throughout the country.

Living restoratively is truly a journey, and we all start in different places. Janine looked at her own role and situation and decided to take action. Maybe there is conflict in your workplace or area of ministry. Maybe your family is longing for ways to reconnect with one another. Just know that even small changes can make a big difference in building a culture of hope, redemption, and life!

Considerations for Restorative Practices

As we engage in activities to promote restorative justice, it is critical to include those who are most directly impacted throughout the process. When we imagine various ways to create change and consider the unique needs of different communities and cultures, we will find that restorative practices look different depending on the particular setting. What works in one place may not work in another, but we can be inspired by and learn from experiences of others and then, looking to our own traditions and cultures, create encounter that is even more applicable and, therefore, transformative.

We all have different passions and interests, different backgrounds and relationships, different social locations, experiences, and political perspectives. These varieties of gifts make us one in the Body of Christ. All are needed to promote restorative justice. As you read about examples of restorative justice in action, notice what stands out to you, what idea sticks in your mind as you fall asleep, or what image you continue to think about in the coming weeks and months. Pay attention to these things, pray about them, research them further, and talk with others. You never know what inspiration or opportunity may arise.

Community Ministries and Programs

Throughout this book you have seen references to Catholic programs that use restorative practices to transform the criminal justice system and the lives of those it affects. Bridges To Life is an organization that works "to connect communities to prisons in an effort to reduce the recidivism rate (particularly that resulting from violent crimes), reduce the number of crime victims, and enhance public safety."[2] John Sage founded the organization after his sister was killed. This fourteen-week program combines restorative dialogue between survivors and perpetrators of similar crimes with spiritual reflection, story-telling, and life-skills training to create a holistic and transformative experience for all involved.

Precious Blood Ministry of Reconciliation is a community-based ministry in Chicago that "reach[es] out to the victim, the wrongdoer, and the community to create a safe space where healing can begin and where people can find the support and encouragement needed to begin reconciliation."[3] Among many programs, they hold circles for those impacted by violence in their neighborhood. Meanwhile, in California, parishes throughout the state have trained circle keepers who host support groups for those impacted by crime and incarceration.

As a secular organization, Restorative Response Baltimore[4] receives referrals from schools and the juvenile justice system to facilitate dialogues that help to prevent youth from serving suspensions, expulsions, or a prison sentence. In the Minnesota Department of Corrections, victim-initiated restorative practices are built into their system. These include opportunities for dialogue as well as an apology letter exchange.[5] Initiatives like this exist in many parts of the country and seek volunteers to be facilitators. This is a great way to become trained and directly involved in restorative practices.

Many of these secular programs recognize the vital role of faith communities in supporting those impacted by violence.

See if some of these initiatives exist in your city or state and reach out to ask how your parish or ministry can collaborate. To help others in your community learn more, invite representatives from these programs to speak at an event.

Political Advocacy

While it is not always possible to become actively involved in a restorative justice program or ministry, we can each play a role in influencing policy. Stay informed about what is happening in the local, state, and federal criminal justice system. When you hear about a policy or practice that does not honor the dignity of those affected by crime, speak up by calling or writing to your state representatives or members of Congress, write a letter to the editor of your local paper, or assist with voter education.

Catholic Mobilizing Network was formed to work toward ending the use of the death penalty in the United States and to promote restorative justice. To carry out an execution is to take away that person's basic right to life and remove any possibility of redemption. Meanwhile, it does not meet victims' needs for healing and only continues a cycle of violence and suffering. The death penalty is the most extreme form of retribution in our society, and it is unnecessary, immoral, and contrary to the Gospel. To get involved in education, advocacy, and prayer to end capital punishment, sign the National Catholic Pledge to End the Death Penalty (www.catholicsmobilizing.org). Ordinary Catholics can have a powerful impact in advocating for death penalty repeal in states with the practice, making calls for clemency in upcoming executions, and utilizing education and prayer resources in their communities.

The death penalty is the tip of the iceberg in a criminal justice system that harms instead of heals. Other policy issues that contribute to creating a more restorative system include ending mandatory minimum sentencing, increasing access to drug treatment, job training, and mental health services; and ensuring access to victims' services and involvement in proceedings. In what ways can your state or local criminal justice system better prioritize healing and human dignity over punishment?

Rehabilitative Programs

In many areas of the country there are ministries and programs that attend to the spiritual and corporal needs of those who are currently or formerly incarcerated. Whether offering a ministry of accompaniment, spiritual support, housing services, or job placement, these components can play a vital role in helping someone take responsibility, make personal changes, and meet basic needs in order to thrive upon release. These spiritual and rehabilitative components can be powerful contributors to successful reintegration to community life. **Restorative practices can be infused in these ministries and allow individuals to repair relationships with those they have harmed, family, or their community.**

Pope Francis says it beautifully:

> To me, this seems to be the great challenge that we all must face together, so that the measures adopted against evil are not satisfied by restraining, dissuading, and isolating the many who have caused it, but also helps them to reflect, to travel the paths of good, to be authentic persons who, removed from their own hardships, become merciful themselves. The Church, therefore, proposes a humanizing, genuinely reconciling justice, a justice that leads the criminal, through educational development and brave atonement, to rehabilitation and reintegration into the community.[6]

Restorative circles can be especially useful in such ministries. Beyond facilitating dialogue between victims and offenders, they can be used with groups of currently or formerly incarcerated individuals to heal trauma, elicit accountability, and contemplate ways to make amends for their actions. In addition, parishes can create ministries of support and reintegration for individuals who are leaving prison. Whether using circles in prison-based ministry or another setting, Catholic Mobilizing Network's website has more information about how to find training opportunities.

Find a Circle Trainer
For many Catholics, after learning about the principles and practices of restorative justice, they wish to become trained in circle keeping. CMN's dedicated webpage offers discerning questions and suggested organizations experienced in conducting circle trainings with faith communities. Find a link to the page at www.catholicsmobilizing .org/rj-reader-guide.

Truth-Telling and Racial Healing

The last chapter offered an overview of ways that racism is manifested in our criminal justice system. In the bishops' recent pastoral letter against racism, they insist:

> Too many good and faithful Catholics remain unaware of the connection between institutional racism and the continued erosion of the sanctity of life. We are not finished with the work. The evil of racism festers in part because, as a nation, there has been very limited formal acknowledgement of the harm

done to so many, no moment of atonement, no national process of reconciliation and, all too often a neglect of our history. Many of our institutions still harbor, and too many of our laws still sanction, practices that deny justice and equal access to certain groups of people. God demands more from us. We cannot, therefore, look upon the progress against racism in recent decades and conclude that our current situation meets the standard of justice. In fact, God demands what is right and just.[7]

The bishops go on to describe that lynching is an example of systemic violence that "must be fully recognized and addressed in any process that hopes to combat racism."[8] Some people are surprised to learn that there is a direct connection between lynching and the death penalty in America.[9] Working toward its abolition not only honors the human dignity of those sentenced to death, but rids our nation of an explicitly racist practice. Whether lynching and the death penalty, slavery and mass incarceration, genocide and marginalization of native peoples, or rejection of immigrants, we must find ways to openly talk about harms committed against people of color in the United States, both in the past and the present. Informed by such truth-telling, we can more effectively change behaviors, systems, and structures that violate human dignity based on a person's skin color.

Thinking and talking about our country in this way may be difficult. It requires us to recognize the ways in which we are part of unjust structures and to make conscious changes in how we engage with one another. A restorative justice approach can help us in this long journey. Parishes throughout the country are using circles to hold difficult conversations about race and privilege in America and discern future action. Numerous Catholic universities and religious communities are taking steps to make amends for slavery, segregation, and other racist actions in their past or present. How can restorative practices play a role in your parish and community's response to racial injustice?

In Our Institutions

As you think about ways you can create a more restorative culture, consider the places you naturally find yourself—your school, your workplace, your parish community. What policies or processes are in place to address harm or discipline? It was mentioned earlier how restorative dialogue is being used more and more in schools. Not only is this a natural place to teach skills for healthy and productive conflict resolution at an early age, but these approaches are also actually helping to break down what has been called the "school-to-prison pipeline." Research shows that when children are suspended or expelled, they are more likely to find themselves in prison later in life.[10] Removing kids from their learning environment has a detrimental effect on their development and behavior. Then, continued "acting out" can escalate to violent behavior in or outside of school that results in arrest. By using restorative practices that allow young people to understand the effects of their actions on others at a critical time in their development, while including parents, teachers, and administrators in the process, all are able to continue learning, growing, and integrating healthy habits for conflict resolution in mutually supportive ways.

In our workplaces, a small rift or personality difference can fester to become a major problem. Perhaps your line of work is highly stressful, or you provide services to individuals who have experienced trauma. Restorative practices can serve to resolve conflict between colleagues and clients, create spaces for support and self-care, and bring healing to those who have suffered harm.

Finally, in many ways, our parish communities wrestle with internal conflict, work to address injustice in society, or struggle to respond to an instance of harm within the community. Here are a few ideas for ways that parishes can integrate restorative principles to be spaces of welcome, healing, and justice. Use circles for community building and holding difficult conversations. (Having members of the parish who are trained in circle process may be particularly helpful.) Cultivate the spirit of inclusion when making decisions. In other words, make sure that those most affected by an issue have a say in the outcome. Create ministries of support for individuals impacted by the criminal justice system—victims of crime, individuals who are incarcerated, and the families of both. Finally, educate others about issues of criminal justice and church teaching on restorative justice.

CMN's Small Group Modules
Catholic Mobilizing Network developed *Restorative Justice, Restorative Living* for small groups to learn about restorative justice, consider how it connects to our Catholic faith, and discern ways to put it into action. To learn more, visit: www.catholicsmobilizing.org/rj-reader-guide

In Our Everyday Lives

Throughout this book, you have reflected on ways in which your own life is affected by the criminal justice system. For each person reading, that relationship is different, although one thing we share in common is that a culture of retribution and punishment pervades our everyday lives. Timothy Wolfe puts it this way in *Redemption and Restoration*: "Because all of these problems are interrelated and symptomatic of larger underlying problems, simply addressing one or even a few aspects of our broken criminal justice system will not be sufficient. We need change that is broad and deep. In order to properly change practices and policies, we need to change hearts and minds."[11]

Often, this change happens through experience. There is a reason why they are called restorative *practices*. The more we examine the consequences of our actions, seek out opportunities for dialogue, and collaborate to make things right again, the sooner this becomes a natural way of being in relationship with one another. When we model this restorative way of being with our day-to-day actions, then others experience the power of encounter that is rooted in hope, healing, and human dignity.

The best place to start might be in your own family. Many families, in various stages of life, use circles to reconnect with one another in the busyness of life or address an area of hardship or conflict. Getting started can be simple, such as sharing a joy or challenge of the day around the dinner table. Then, when a more difficult topic needs to be addressed, you can revisit the questions: What was the harm? Who was impacted and how? What needs to be done to make it right?

As We Go Forth

There is such great brokenness in our criminal justice system and there are so many ways that Catholics can contribute to transforming it. By becoming agents of restoration, we uplift the human dignity of *all* those impacted by crime, especially those who have suffered harm. Without opportunities to repair people and relationships impacted by crime, too often suffering manifests in further violence. Through use of restorative practices, we interrupt these destructive cycles, healing past harms and helping to prevent future ones. In taking up this call, we proclaim a vision for reconciling justice in a hurting world.

By continuing to reflect on and pray about the call to restorative justice, we recognize when we are responsible for causing harm to others, are in need of healing ourselves, and can be a light of hope in a hurting world. When Pope Francis spoke at the Curran-Fromhold Correctional Facility, he addressed the need for rehabilitation in the lives of those incarcerated, but he also called every person to recognize the ways in which our humanity, our suffering, and our redemption are bound up together. Furthermore, he reminded us that the Lord leads us on our journey toward restoration. And so, we conclude with his words:

> Life means "getting our feet dirty" from the dust-filled roads of life and history. All of us need to be cleansed, to be washed. All of us are being sought out by the Teacher, who wants to help us resume our journey. The Lord goes in search of us; to all of us he stretches out a helping hand. It is painful when we see prison systems which are not concerned to care for wounds, to soothe pain, to offer new possibilities. It is painful when we see people who think that only others need to be cleansed, purified, and do not recognize that their weariness, pain and wounds are also the weariness, pain and wounds of society. The Lord tells us this clearly with a sign: he washes our feet so we can come back to the table. The table

from which he wishes no one to be excluded. The table which is spread for all and to which all of us are invited.[11]

Prayer

Join tens of thousands of faithful people in praying Catholic Mobilizing Network's prayer. We prepare our hearts and embolden our shared education and advocacy to end the death penalty and promote restorative justice in the United States.

God of Mercy, you bestow upon every person a dignity that cannot be extinguished, no matter the harm someone has suffered or caused. Rooted in this sacred value of all life, we work together to transform the criminal justice system by ending the death penalty. Enliven our commitment to "work with determination for its abolition worldwide." Ignite in our imaginations more restorative approaches to harm and violence that embody your vision of right relationship. For any person who is a victim of, responsible for, or witness to crime, may we be vessels of your hope, healing, and redemption. Enkindle in us the fire to foster a culture of life. Sustain our pursuit of reconciling justice, that we may model your compassion and mercy with our lives. In Jesus' name we pray. Amen.

Reflection Questions:

1. Think about a ministry in your parish or community that you're involved in: catechetical instruction, liturgical ministry, community outreach. . . . How could it be more restorative in nature?

2. Call to mind one of your favorite Scripture passages. Can you think of a way in which it calls Christians and people of faith to live restoratively?

3. After reading through this chapter, what is one action that you commit to taking to promote restorative justice in your community?

Glossary

alternative sentencing—When restorative practices are used in collaboration with the formal criminal justice system (most frequently in juvenile cases) to determine an agreement that does not result in prison time for the perpetrator.

Catholic Catechism revision on the death penalty (number 2267)—On August 2, 2018, the Congregation for the Doctrine of the Faith released revised language on the Catholic Church's position on capital punishment, saying that "'the death penalty is inadmissible because it is an attack on the inviolability and dignity of the person,' and she works with determination for its abolition worldwide." To read the full revised text of paragraph number 2267, analysis, and previous papal statements on the death penalty, visit https://catholicsmobilizing.org/church-speaks /catechism-revision-death-penalty-inadmissible.

Catholic Mobilizing Network—Catholic Mobilizing Network is a national organization that mobilizes Catholics and all people of goodwill to value life over death, to end the use of the death penalty, to transform the US criminal justice system from punitive to restorative, and to build capacity in US society to engage in restorative practices. Through education, advocacy, and prayer, and based on the Gospel value that every human is created in the image and likeness of God, CMN expresses the fundamental belief that all those who have caused or been impacted by crime should be treated with dignity. CMN works in close collaboration with the United States Conference of Catholic Bishops and lives the Spirit of Unity of its sponsor, the Congregation of St. Joseph. To learn more and get involved, visit www .catholicsmobilizing.org.

circles (also called peacemaking circles, healing circles, or circle process)—A restorative practice in which individuals sit in a circle and pass a talking piece around to designate the speaker. Participants each respond to a prompt or question, going around the circle in order without interruptions. Circles are highly versatile and may be described differently depending on the purpose and environment in which they are used.

community/family members/support people—The person or persons who were indirectly impacted by the crime or incident of harm. These individuals are included in restorative justice because we are all interconnected in a web of relationships.

culture of encounter—Throughout his papacy Pope Francis has encouraged the faithful to reach out beyond one's usual circles and to make a point of encountering people who are on the margins of society. This concept requires a posture of mercy (another key concept of Pope Francis's pontificate) rather than judgment. Pope Francis uses this concept in stark contrast to the "throwaway culture," where people who are marginalized, such as the elderly, the sick, the poor, and the incarcerated, are often ignored or considered disposable.[1]

offender/perpetrator/responsible party—The person or persons who cause a crime or incident of harm. Every person is more than the worst thing they have ever done. Individuals have different preferences for how they describe their role in relation to the harm they were a part.

restorative encounter—Formal or informal interactions that repair relationships and bring healing to those impacted by harm. An informal encounter might be friends, family members, or colleagues talking openly about an instance of harm and taking steps toward making amends.

restorative justice process—Refers to restorative practices in which all three parties (victim, offender, and community) are involved.

restorative practices—Particular types of encounter such as circles or victim-offender dialogue that are more formal in nature. These may involve all three parties, but could also involve only one party (such as in a victim support circle) or two parties (offender and community reentry circle).

trauma—A term used to broadly describe adverse or harmful experiences that go beyond a person's regular ability to cope. This may be a single event, or prolonged period of abuse or distress. Restorative practices can play a meaningful role in trauma healing, but it is also important that they are carried out in a way that does not retraumatize participants.[2]

victim-offender dialogue (also called restorative conferencing)—A facilitated meeting that brings together person(s) who caused a harm, person(s) who suffered the harm, and community members to discuss the impacts of the incident and what needs to be done to make it right.

victim/survivor/harmed party—The person or persons who directly suffered from a crime or incident of harm. Every person is more than the worst thing they have ever suffered and individuals have different preferences for how they describe their identity in relation to the harm they experienced.

Notes

Chapter 1

1. Letter of Pope Francis to Participants in the 19th International Congress of the International Association of Penal Law and of the 3rd Congress of the Latin-American Association of Penal Law and Criminology (May 30, 2014) 3; https://w2.vatican.va/content/francesco /en/letters/2014/documents/papa-francesco_20140530_lettera -diritto-penale-criminologia.html.

2. Matthew W. Epperson and Carrie Pettus-Davis, "Smart Decarceration: Guiding Concepts for an Era of Criminal Justice Transformation," Center for Social Development at Washington University in St. Louis (2015), 2.

3. Executive Office of the President of the United States, "Economic Perspectives on Incarceration and the Criminal Justice System" (2016), 7; https://obamawhitehouse.archives.gov/sites/default/files /page/files/20160423_cea_incarceration_criminal_justice.pdf. See also Bureau of Justice Statistics, "Employment and Expenditure," https://www.bjs.gov/index.cfm?ty=tp&tid=5; and Michael Mitchell and Michael Leachman, "Changing Priorities: State Criminal Justice Reforms and Investments in Education," Center on Budget and Policy Priorities (October 28, 2014), http://www.cbpp.org/research /changing-priorities-state-criminal-justice-reforms-and-investments -in-education.

4. CDF, instruction, *Donum vitae*, intro. 5; quoted in *Catechism of the Catholic Church*, 2nd ed. (United States Catholic Conference–Libreria Editrice Vaticana, 1997), 2258.

5. United States Conference of Catholic Bishops, *Responsibility, Rehabilitation, and Restoration: A Catholic Perspective on Crime and Criminal Justice* (Washington, DC: USCCB, 2000). The text is also available in *Origins* 30, no. 25 (November 30, 2000): 389, 391–404; and on the USCCB website: www.usccb.org/issues-and-action/human-life-and-dignity/criminal-justice-restorative-justice/crime-and-criminal-justice.cfm.

6. Trudy D. Conway, David Matzko McCarthy, and Vicki Schieber, eds., *Redemption and Restoration: A Catholic Perspective on Restorative Justice* (Collegeville, MN: Liturgical Press, 2017), 103.

7. Conway, McCarthy, and Schieber, eds., *Redemption and Restoration*, 143–45.

8. Francis, *Evangelii Gaudium* (Vatican City: Libreria Editrice Vaticana, 2015), 272, http://w2.vatican.va/content/francesco/en/apost_exhortations/documents/papa-francesco_esortazione-ap_20131124_evangelii-gaudium.html.

9. Kay Pranis, *The Little Book of Circle Process: A New/Old Approach to Peacemaking* (Intercourse, PA: Good Books, 2005).

10. Howard Zehr, *The Little Book of Victim Offender Conferencing: Bringing Victims and Offenders Together in Dialogue* (Intercourse, PA: Good Books, 2009).

Chapter 2

1. Lorenn Walker, "Restorative Justice: Definition and Purpose," in *Restorative Justice Today: Practical Applications*, ed. Katherine S. van Wormer and Lorenn Walker, 3–4 (Los Angeles: Sage Publications, 2013). Walker notes that Jane's story is "loosely based on real incidents" (4).

2. Conway, McCarthy, and Schieber, eds., *Redemption and Restoration*, 55.

3. Carolyn Yoder, *The Little Book of Trauma Healing* (Intercourse, PA: Good Books, 2005).

4. Letter of Pope Francis to Participants in the 19th International Congress of the International Association of Penal Law and of the 3rd Congress of the Latin-American Association of Penal Law and Criminology.

5. *Responsibility, Rehabilitation, and Restoration,* http://www.usccb
.org/issues-and-action/human-life-and-dignity/criminal-justice
-restorative-justice/crime-and-criminal-justice.cfm.

6. Conway, McCarthy, and Schieber, eds., *Redemption and Restoration,* 162.

7. Desmond Tutu, *No Future without Forgiveness* (New York: Image, 2000), 272.

Chapter 3

1. Conway, McCarthy, and Schieber, eds., *Redemption and Restoration,* 92.

2. Conway, McCarthy, and Schieber, eds., *Redemption and Restoration,* 93.

3. *Catechism of the Catholic Church,* 2267.

4. This account is included in more detail in *Redemption and Restoration.* Additional information was included from Peter Rowe, "Senseless Violence, Unbelievable Forgiveness: The Tariq Khamisa Foundation," *The San Diego Union-Tribune,* October 8, 2016, http://www
.sandiegouniontribune.com/lifestyle/people/sd-me-tariq-assembly
-20161007-htmlstory.html.

5. Susan Sharpe, PhD, "Catholic Social Teaching and Restorative Justice," https://catholicsmobilizing.org/catholic-social-teaching
-restorative-justice.

6. Frank R. Baumgartner, Derek A. Epp, and Bayard Love, "Police Searches of Black and White Motorists," UNC-Chapel Hill (August 5, 2014), http://fbaum.unc.edu/TrafficStops/DrivingWhileBlack
-BaumgartnerLoveEpp-August2014.pdf.

7. Conway, McCarthy, and Schieber, eds., *Redemption and Restoration,* 50.

8. The Sentencing Project, http://www.sentencingproject.org/issues
/racial-disparity/.

9. Richard Rohr, *Things Hidden: Scripture as Spirituality* (Franciscan Media: 2008), 24–25.

10. Pope Francis' Speech to Prisoners at the Curran-Fromhold Correctional Facility (September 27, 2015), https://6abc.com/religion/pope
-francis-speech-to-prisoners-at-curran-fromhold-correctional-facility
/1004577/.

Chapter 4

1. Conway, McCarthy, and Schieber, eds., *Redemption and Restoration*, 23.

2. Francis, *Laudato Si'* (Vatican City: Libreria Editrice Vaticana, 2015), 137, http://w2.vatican.va/content/francesco/en/encyclicals/documents/papa-francesco_20150524_enciclica-laudato-si.html.

3. Tutu, *No Future without Forgiveness*, 31.

4. USCCB, "Seven Themes of Catholic Social Teaching," http://www.usccb.org/beliefs-and-teachings/what-we-believe/catholic-social-teaching/seven-themes-of-catholic-social-teaching.cfm. The list originates in the US Catholic bishops' *Sharing Catholic Social Teaching: Challenges and Directions* (Washington, DC: United States Catholic Conference, 1998), 4–6.

5. Conway, McCarthy, and Schieber, eds., *Redemption and Restoration*, 128.

6. Bureau of Justice Statistics, "U.S. Prison Population Declined by One Percent in 2014" (September 17, 2015), https://www.bjs.gov/content/pub/press/p14pr.cfm.

7. ACLU, "The Prison Crisis," https://www.aclu.org/prison-crisis.

8. Executive Office of the President, "Economic Perspectives on Incarceration," 43.

9. National Archives, *The Constitution: Amendments 11–27*, https://www.archives.gov/founding-docs/amendments-11-27.

10. Michelle Alexander, *The New Jim Crow: Mass Incarceration in the Age of Colorblindness*, rev. ed. (New York: New Press, 2012).

11. Conway, McCarthy, and Schieber, eds., *Redemption and Restoration*, 189.

12. *Rite of Penance*, 5, in *The Rites of the Catholic Church: Volume One* (Collegeville, MN: Liturgical Press, 1990).

13. Catholic News Service, "Mass Formally Opens Canonization Cause for Chief Black Elk," November 2, 2017.

14. John Neihardt, *Black Elk Speaks: The Complete Edition* (Lincoln, NE: University of Nebraska Press, 2014), 121.

Chapter 5

1. Conway, McCarthy, and Schieber, eds., *Redemption and Restoration*, 35.

2. Bridges To Life, "History and Mission," www.bridgestolife.org /index.php?option=com_content&view=article&id=3&Itemid=6.

3. Precious Blood Ministry of Reconciliation, "Our Ministries," https://pbmr.org/ministries/.

4. Restorative Response Baltimore, https://www.restorativeresponse .org/.

5. Minnesota Department of Corrections, "Restorative Justice," https://mn.gov/doc/victims/restorative-justice/.

6. Letter of Pope Francis to Participants in the 19th International Congress of the International Association of Penal Law and of the 3rd Congress of the Latin-American Association of Penal Law and Criminology.

7. United States Conference of Catholic Bishops, *Open Wide Our Hearts: The Enduring Call to Love, A Pastoral Letter Against Racism* (Washington, DC: USCCB, 2018), 10. The text is available on the USCCB website: http://www.usccb.org/issues-and-action/human-life -and-dignity/racism/index.cfm.

8. USCCB, *Open Wide Our Hearts*, 15.

9. Equal Justice Initiative, *Lynching in America: Confronting the Legacy of Racial Terror*, https://lynchinginamerica.eji.org/report/.

10. Fania Davis, "Discipline With Dignity: Oakland Classrooms Try Healing Instead of Punishment," *Yes! Magazine* (March 7, 2014), https:// truthout.org/articles/discipline-with-dignity-oakland-classrooms -try-healing-instead-of-punishment/.

11. Conway, McCarthy, and Schieber, eds., *Redemption and Restoration*, 46.

12. Pope Francis' Speech to Prisoners at the Curran-Fromhold Correctional Facility (September 27, 2015).

Glossary

1. These themes are discussed further in the apostolic exhortation *Evangelii Gaudium*. Full text can be found at: http://w2.vatican.va/content/francesco/en/apost_exhortations/documents/papa-francesco_esortazione-ap_20131124_evangelii-gaudium.html.

2. Carolyn Yoder, *The Little Book of Trauma Healing* (Intercourse, PA: Good Books, 2005).